Mel Bay's Modern
GUITAR METHOD
GRADE 7
Expanded Edition

1 2 3 4 5 6 7 8 9 0

© 2008 BY MEL BAY PUBLICATIONS, INC., PACIFIC, MO 63069.
ALL RIGHTS RESERVED. INTERNATIONAL COPYRIGHT SECURED. B.M.I. MADE AND PRINTED IN U.S.A.
No part of this publication may be reproduced in whole or in part, or stored in a retrieval system, or transmitted in any form
or by any means, electronic, mechanical, photocopy, recording, or otherwise, without written permission of the publisher.

Visit us on the Web at www.melbay.com — E-mail us at email@melbay.com

Key of C Review

Open Position

2nd Position

5th Position

7th Position

© 2008 Mel Bay Publications (BMI). All Rights Reserved.

Key of Am Review

Open Position

2nd Position

5th Position

9th Position

© 2008 Mel Bay Publications (BMI). All Rights Reserved.

Key of G Review

Open Position

2nd Position

7th Position

9th Position

© 2008 Mel Bay Publications (BMI). All Rights Reserved.

Key of Em Review

Open Position

4th Position

7th Position

9th Position

© 2008 Mel Bay Publications (BMI). All Rights Reserved.

Key of F Review

1st Position

5th Position

7th Position

10th Position

© 2008 Mel Bay Publications (BMI). All Rights Reserved.

Key of Dm Review

Open Position

5th Position

7th Position

10th Position

© 2008 Mel Bay Publications (BMI). All Rights Reserved.

Key of D Review

2nd Position

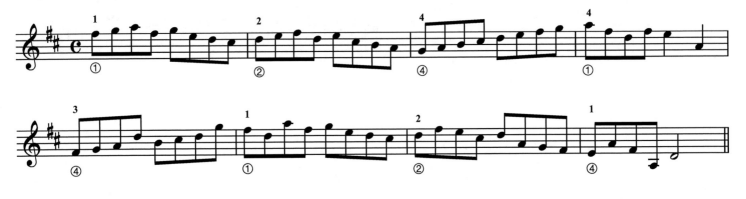

4th Position

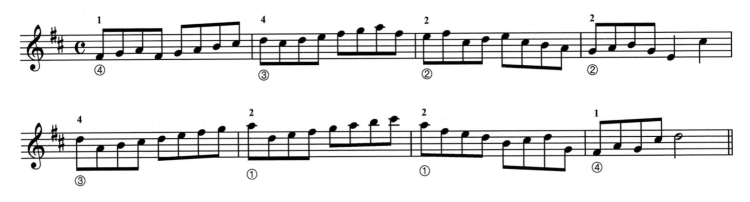

7th Position

9th Position

© 2008 Mel Bay Publications (BMI). All Rights Reserved.

Key of Bm Review

2nd Position

4th Position

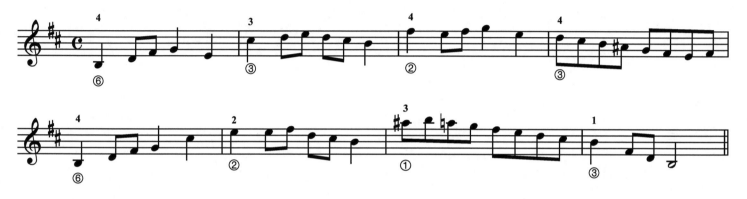

7th Position

11th Position

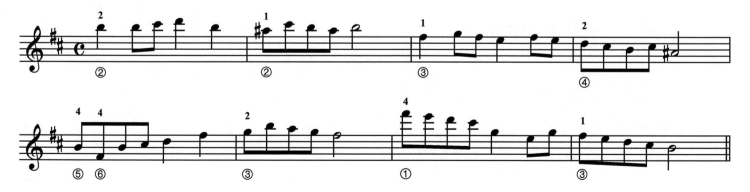

© 2008 Mel Bay Publications (BMI). All Rights Reserved.

Key of B♭ Review

Open Position

3rd Position

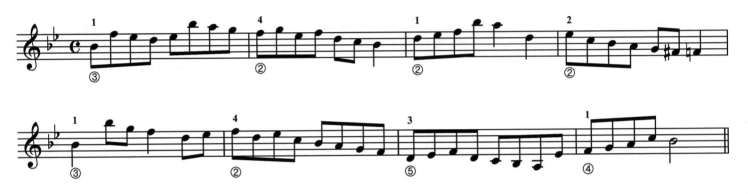

5th Position

10th Position

© 2008 Mel Bay Publications (BMI). All Rights Reserved.

10

Key of Gm Review

Open Position

3rd Position

7th Position

10th Position

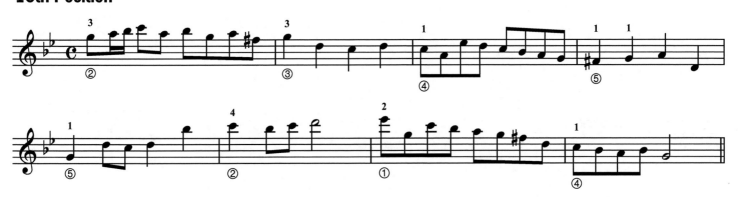

© 2008 Mel Bay Publications (BMI). All Rights Reserved.

Key of A Review

Open Position

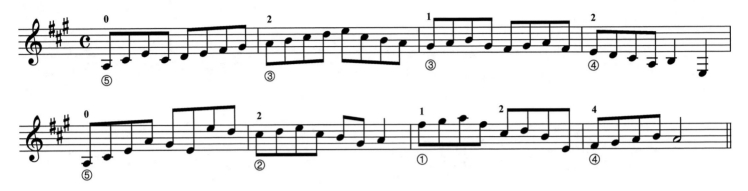

2nd Position

4th Position

9th Position

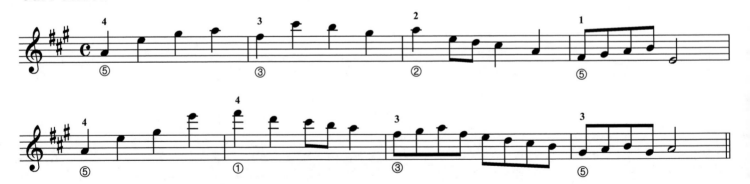

© 2008 Mel Bay Publications (BMI). All Rights Reserved.

Key of F#m Review

2nd Position

6th Position

9th Position

11th Position

© 2008 Mel Bay Publications (BMI). All Rights Reserved.

Key of E♭ Review

3rd Position

5th Position

8th Position

10th Position

© 2008 Mel Bay Publications (BMI). All Rights Reserved.

Key of Cm Review

Open Position

3rd Position

5th Position

8th Position

© 2008 Mel Bay Publications (BMI). All Rights Reserved.

Key of E Review

Open Position

4th Position

6th Position

9th Position

© 2008 Mel Bay Publications (BMI). All Rights Reserved.

Key of C#m Review

1st Position

4th Position

6th Position

9th Position

© 2008 Mel Bay Publications (BMI). All Rights Reserved.

Key of A♭ Review

1st Position

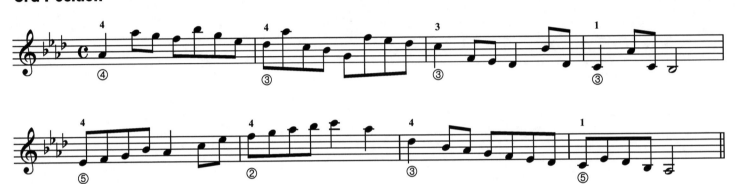

3rd Position

8th Position

10th Position

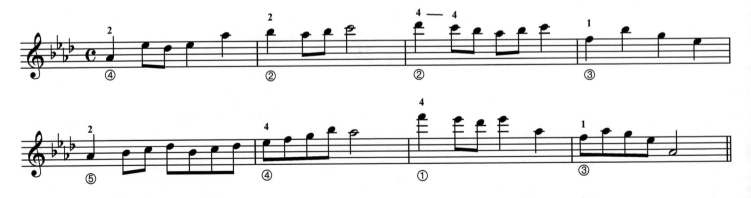

© 2008 Mel Bay Publications (BMI). All Rights Reserved.

18

Key of Fm Review

1st Position

5th Position

8th Position

10th Position

© 2008 Mel Bay Publications (BMI). All Rights Reserved.

The Sea of Recollection

Dropped D Tuning

W. Bay

© 2008 Mel Bay Publications (BMI). All Rights Reserved.

The Key of B Major

The key of B has five sharps. There are F#, C#, G#, D#, and A#.

B Scale – 1st Position

Alma – 1st Pos.

W.B.

B Scale – 4th Position

Fairplay – 4th Pos.

W.B.

© 2008 Mel Bay Publications (BMI). All Rights Reserved.

21

Key of B Review

B Scale – 6th Position

Lyric – 6th Pos.

W.B.

B Scale – 11th Position

Bedelia – 11th Pos.

W.B.

© 2008 Mel Bay Publications (BMI). All Rights Reserved.

The Sixth Chords

The sixth chord consists of the first, third, fifth, and sixth notes of the major scale. It is a major chord with the sixth tone added.

Example

The easiest approach to the production of a sixth chord is to **lower the seventh tone of the dominant seventh chord one half step**. The lowered seventh tone automatically becomes the sixth tone of the scale. Practice the chord changes chromatically up the fingerboard until all seventh-chord forms change to sixth-chord forms with ease.

Numbers below the chord forms indicate the chordal tones. The circle in the sixth forms indicate the former position of the seventh tone before lowering.

I7	I6	III7	III6
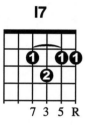	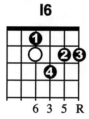	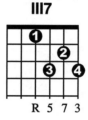	
7 3 5 R	6 3 5 R	R 5 7 3	R 5 6 3

V7	V6	VII7	VI6
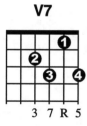	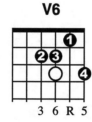	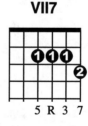	
3 7 R 5	3 6 R 5	5 R 3 7	5 R 3 6

© 2008 Mel Bay Publications (BMI). All Rights Reserved.

The Orchestral Forms of the Sixth Chord

Sixth Chord Etude Number One

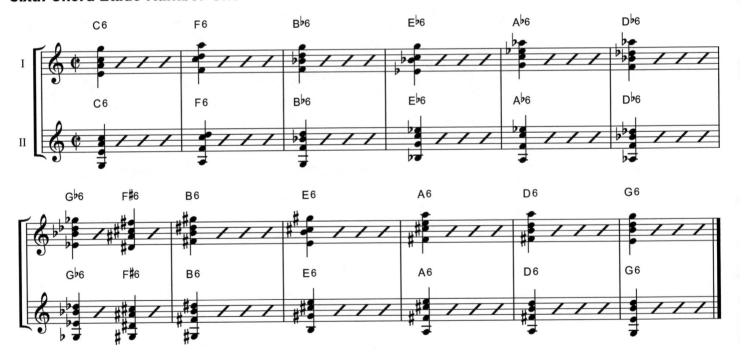

© 2008 Mel Bay Publications (BMI). All Rights Reserved.

My Heart at Thy Sweet Voice

Guitar Duet

Moderato

Saint-Saens
Arr. by Mel Bay

© 2008 Mel Bay Publications (BMI). All Rights Reserved.

Etude in B Major

Guitar Duet

Bertini–Bay

© 2008 Mel Bay Publications (BMI). All Rights Reserved.

Etude in B Major (cont.)

Bertini–Bay

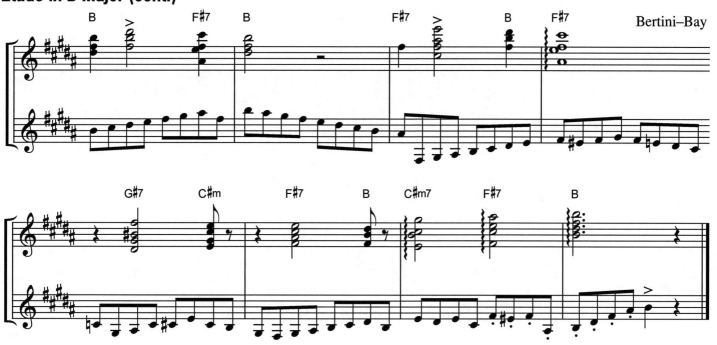

Apollo

W. Bay

© 2008 Mel Bay Publications (BMI). All Rights Reserved.

The Inside Sixth Chord

Sixth Chord Etude Number Two

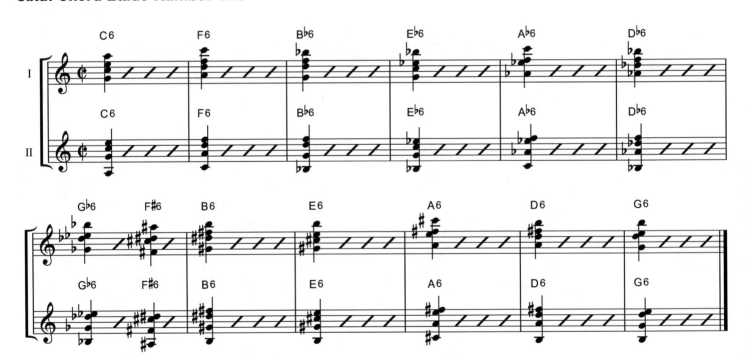

© 2008 Mel Bay Publications (BMI). All Rights Reserved.

The Sixth Chord on the Last Four Strings

Sixth Chord Etude Number Three

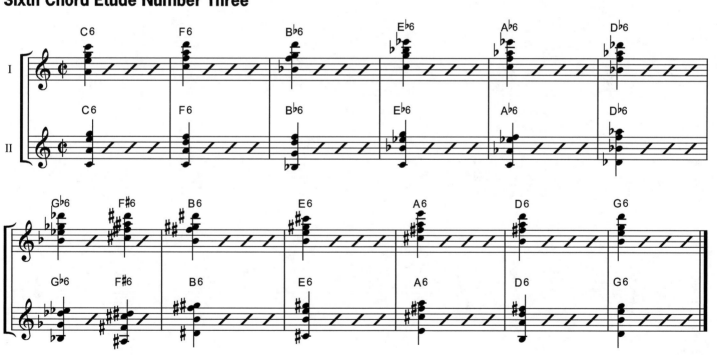

© 2008 Mel Bay Publications (BMI). All Rights Reserved.

Chords in the Key of B

© 2008 Mel Bay Publications (BMI). All Rights Reserved.

B Scale Harmonized

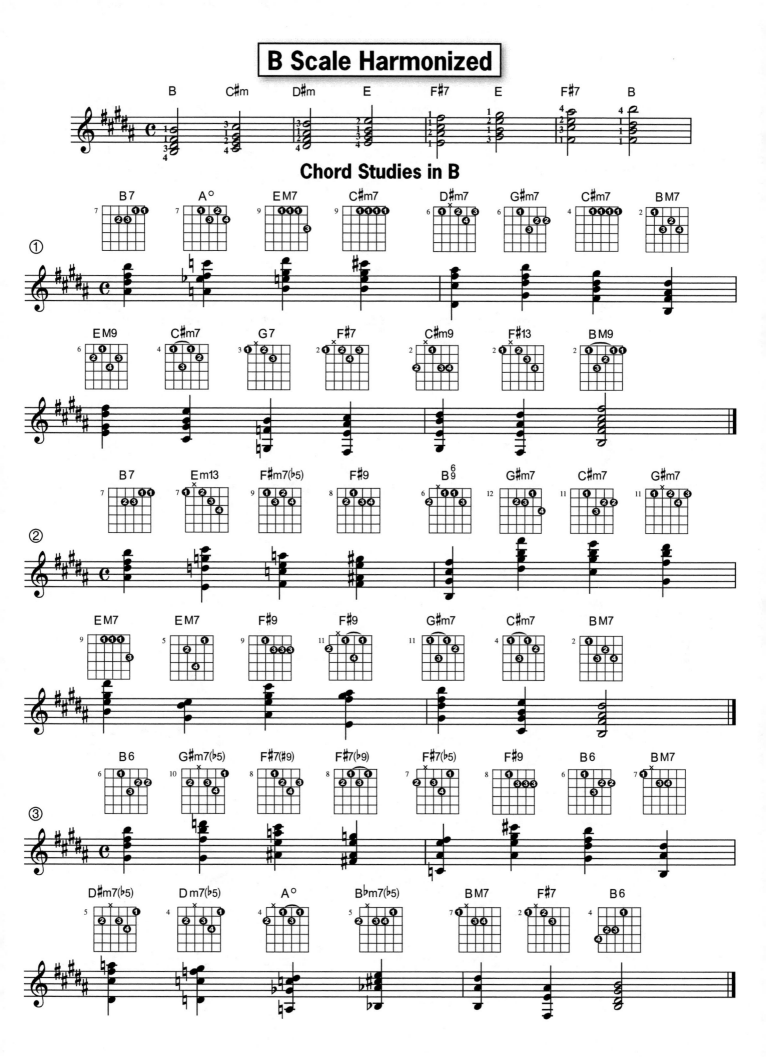

Chord Studies in B

© 2008 Mel Bay Publications (BMI). All Rights Reserved.

© 2008 Mel Bay Publications (BMI). All Rights Reserved.

B Quartal Harmony

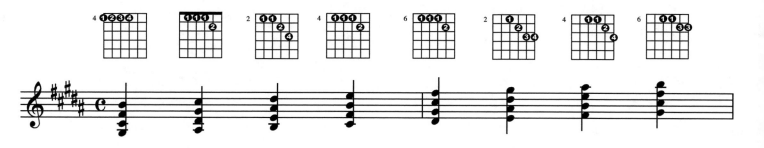

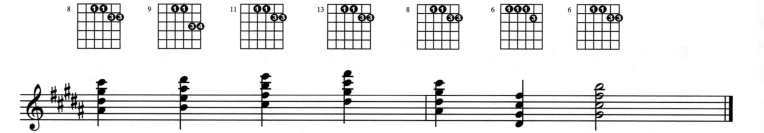

© 2008 Mel Bay Publications (BMI). All Rights Reserved.

33

B Quartal Harmony Studies

© 2008 Mel Bay Publications (BMI). All Rights Reserved.

Key of B Triad Studies

© 2008 Mel Bay Publications (BMI). All Rights Reserved.

The Minor Sixth Chords

The minor sixth chord is made by lowering the third of a sixth a half step. It is commonly referred to as a minor chord with the added sixth.

The Notation of the Minor Sixth Chords

The best procedure for the development of the minor sixth chords is to take each sixth chord form, lower the third, and play the change chromatically up the fingerboard.

© 2008 Mel Bay Publications (BMI). All Rights Reserved.

The Inside Forms of the Minor Sixth Chords

The Minor Sixth Chords on the Last Four Strings

© 2008 Mel Bay Publications (BMI). All Rights Reserved.

The Orchestral Forms of the Minor Sixth Chords

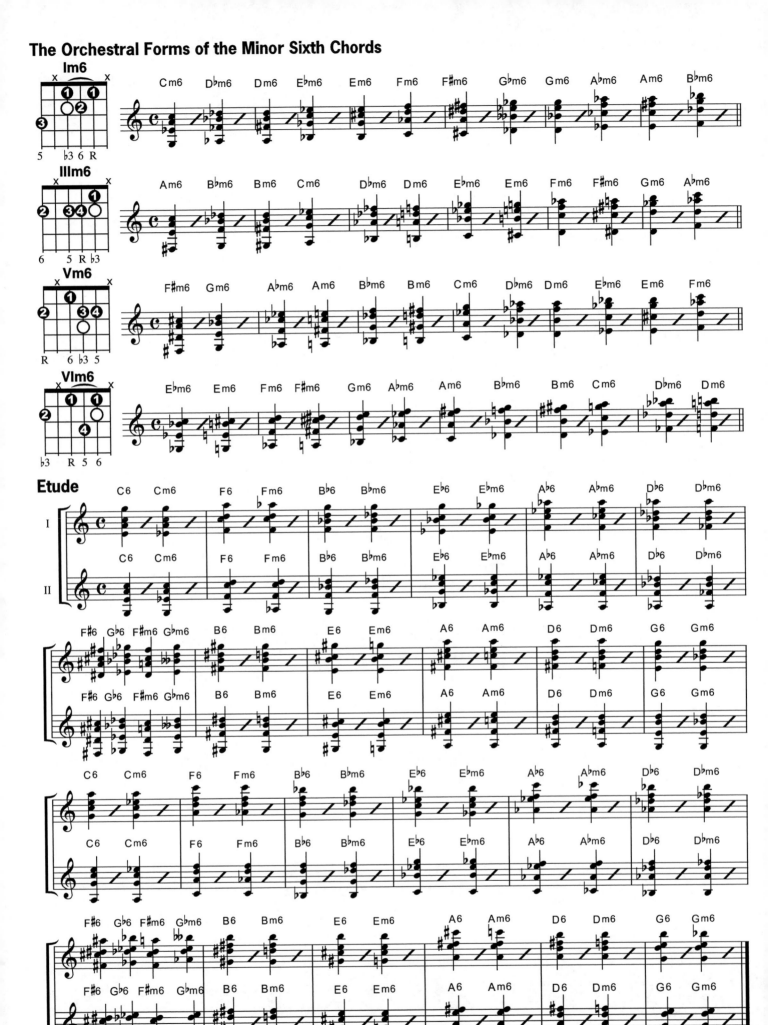

Etude

© 2008 Mel Bay Publications (BMI). All Rights Reserved.

Key of G♯m Review

G Sharp Minor Scale / Harmonic Mode – 1st Position

✕ = Double Sharp

Prologue – 1st Pos.

W.B.

G Sharp Minor Scale / Harmonic Mode – 4th Position

Postlude – 4th Pos.

W.B.

© 2008 Mel Bay Publications (BMI). All Rights Reserved.

Key of G#m Review

G Sharp Minor Scale / Harmonic Mode – 8th Position

Prague – 8th Pos.

W.B.

G Sharp Minor Scale / Harmonic Mode – 11th Position

Vista – 11th Pos.

W.B.

© 2008 Mel Bay Publications (BMI). All Rights Reserved.

Key of G#m Review

1st Position

4th Position

8th Position

11th Position

© 2008 Mel Bay Publications (BMI). All Rights Reserved.

It Is Well with My Soul

Arr. by William Bay

© 2008 Mel Bay Publications (BMI). All Rights Reserved.

It Is Well with my Soul (cont.)

Chico

Guitar Solo

Mel Bay

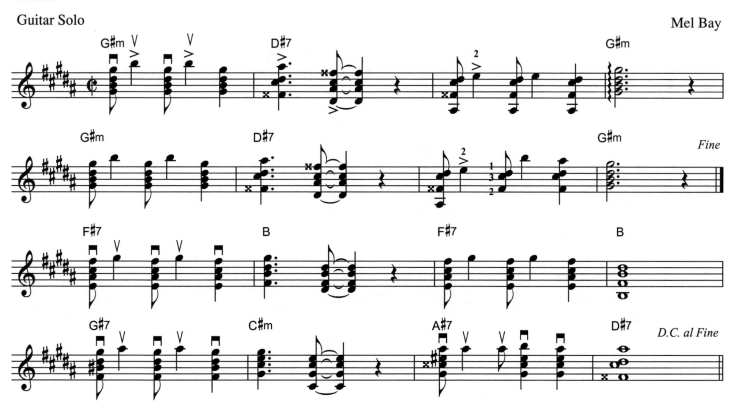

© 2008 Mel Bay Publications (BMI). All Rights Reserved.

Chords in the Key of G#m

© 2008 Mel Bay Publications (BMI). All Rights Reserved.

G#m Scale Harmonized

Chord Studies in G#m

© 2008 Mel Bay Publications (BMI). All Rights Reserved.

© 2008 Mel Bay Publications (BMI). All Rights Reserved.

G#m Quartal Harmony
Using the Pure Minor Scale

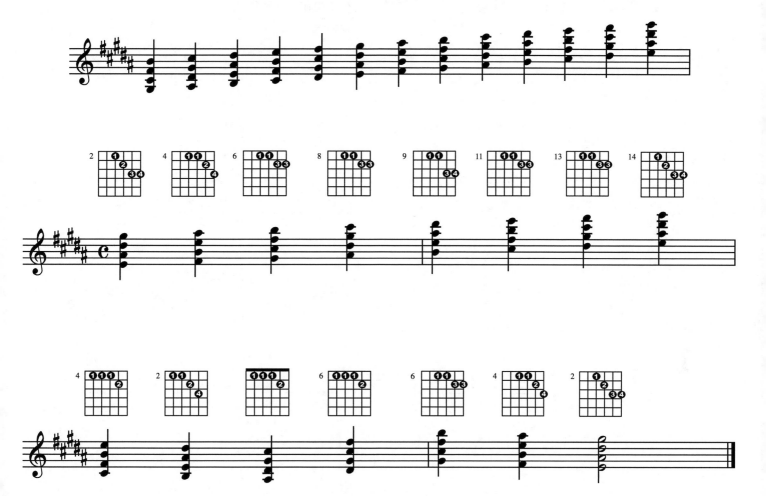

© 2008 Mel Bay Publications (BMI). All Rights Reserved.

G#m Quartal Harmony Studies

© 2008 Mel Bay Publications (BMI). All Rights Reserved.

Key of G#m Triad Studies

© 2008 Mel Bay Publications (BMI). All Rights Reserved.

The Ninth Chords

The ninth chord is a very important chord consisting of the first, third, fifth, a lowered seventh, and a ninth intervals of the major scale. The intervals are root, major third, perfect fifth, minor seventh, and major ninth.

Example

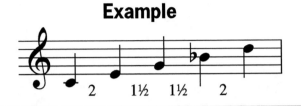

2   1½   1½   2

The Notation of the Ninth Chords

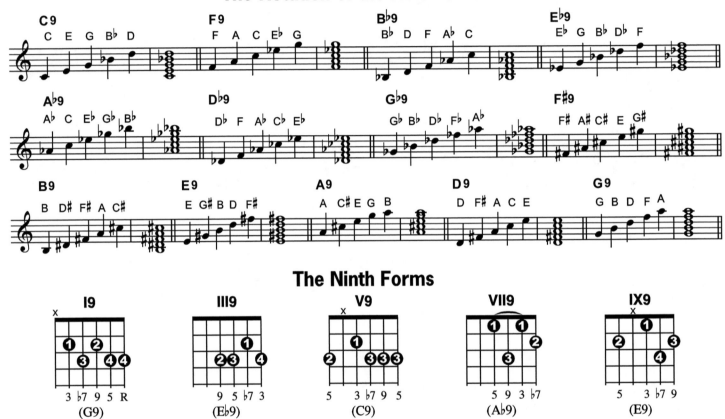

C9   C E G B♭ D

F9   F A C E♭ G

B♭9   B♭ D F A♭ C

E♭9   E♭ G B♭ D♭ F

A♭9   A♭ C E♭ G♭ B♭

D♭9   D♭ F A♭ C♭ E♭

G♭9   G♭ B♭ D♭ F♭ A♭

F♯9   F♯ A♯ C♯ E G♯

B9   B D♯ F♯ A C♯

E9   E G♯ B D F♯

A9   A C♯ E G B

D9   D F♯ A C E

G9   G B D F A

The Ninth Forms

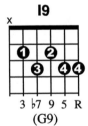

I9
3 ♭7 9 5 R
(G9)

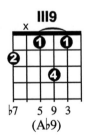

III9
9 5 ♭7 3
(E♭9)

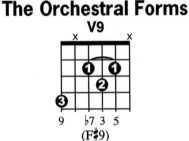

V9
5   3 ♭7 9 5
(C9)

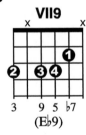

VII9
5 9 3 ♭7
(A♭9)

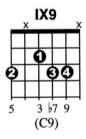

IX9
5   3 ♭7 9
(E9)

The Orchestral Forms

I9
3 ♭7 9 5 R
(G9)

III9
♭7   5 9 3
(A♭9)

V9
9   ♭7 3 5
(F♯9)

VII9
3   9 5 ♭7
(E♭9)

IX9
5   3 ♭7 9
(C9)

*The root has been omitted in forms III9, V9, VII9, and IX9.

An easy way to create a ninth chord on the guitar is to raise the root of a dominant seventh chord one whole step. The root becomes the ninth.

The Altered Ninth Chords

m9 — Lower the 3rd one half step.

9+5 — Raise the 5th one half step.

9♭5 — Lower the 5th one half step.

♭9 — Lower the 9th one half step.

♯9 — Raise the 9th one half step.

m9♭5 — Lower the 3rd and 5th one half step.

♭9♭5 — Lower the 9th and the 5th one half step.

Just As I Am

Dropped D Tuning
Slowly

Hymn
Arr. by William Bay

© 2008 Mel Bay Publications (BMI). All Rights Reserved.

Key of D♭ Review

D Flat Scale – 1st Position

Summer's Day – 1st Pos.

W.B.

D Flat Scale – 3rd Position

Militaire – 3rd Pos.

W.B.

© 2008 Mel Bay Publications (BMI). All Rights Reserved.

Key of D♭ Review

D Flat Scale – 6th Position

Kimmswick – 6th Pos.

W.B.

D Flat Scale – 8th Position

Kearney's Glen – 8th Pos.

W.B.

© 2008 Mel Bay Publications (BMI). All Rights Reserved.

Valse Bluette

R. Drigo
Arr. by Mel Bay

Moderato

© 2008 Mel Bay Publications (BMI). All Rights Reserved.

Valse Bluette (cont.)

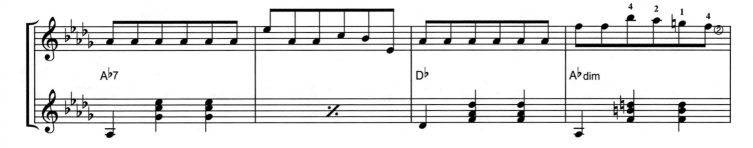

Exercise in D♭ - 8th Position

© 2008 Mel Bay Publications (BMI). All Rights Reserved.

Key of D♭ Review

1st Position

3rd Position

6th Position

8th Position

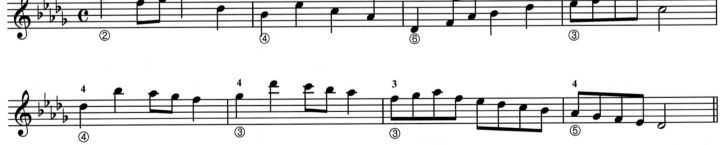

© 2008 Mel Bay Publications (BMI). All Rights Reserved.

Chords in the Key of D♭

© 2008 Mel Bay Publications (BMI). All Rights Reserved.

Db Scale Harmonized

Chord Studies in Db

© 2008 Mel Bay Publications (BMI). All Rights Reserved.

© 2008 Mel Bay Publications (BMI). All Rights Reserved.

D♭ Quartal Harmony

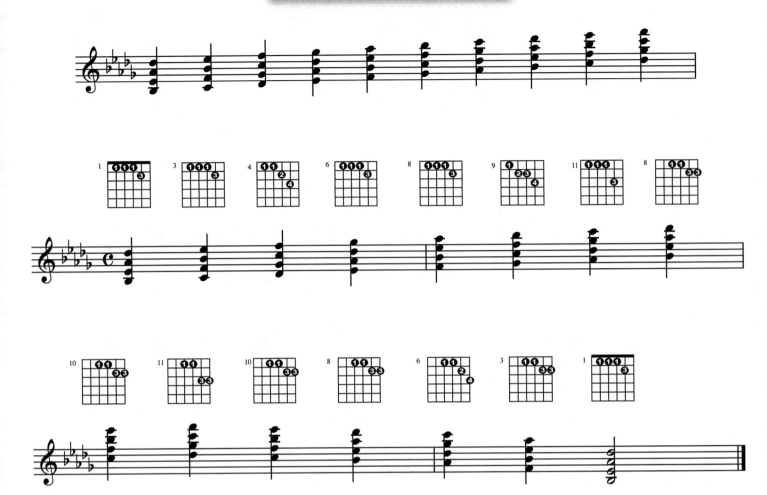

© 2008 Mel Bay Publications (BMI). All Rights Reserved.

D♭ Quartal Harmony Studies

© 2008 Mel Bay Publications (BMI). All Rights Reserved.

The Minute Waltz

Guitar Duet

Molto vivace

F. Chopin
Arr. by Mel Bay

© 2008 Mel Bay Publications (BMI). All Rights Reserved.

The Minute Waltz (cont.)

© 2008 Mel Bay Publications (BMI). All Rights Reserved.

Northern Lights

W. Bay

Freely, flowing

© 2008 Mel Bay Publications (BMI). All Rights Reserved.

Key of D♭ Triad Studies

© 2008 Mel Bay Publications (BMI). All Rights Reserved.

Key of B♭m Review

B Flat Minor Scale / Harmonic Mode – 1st Position

Galaxy – 1st Pos.

W.B.

B Flat Minor Scale / Harmonic Mode – 3rd Position

Night Flight – 3rd Pos.

W.B.

© 2008 Mel Bay Publications (BMI). All Rights Reserved.

Key of B♭m Review

B Flat Minor Scale / Harmonic Mode – 6th Position

Tocatta – 6th Pos.

W.B.

B Flat Minor Scale / Harmonic Mode – 10th Position

Nocturne – 10th Pos.

W.B.

© 2008 Mel Bay Publications (BMI). All Rights Reserved.

Key of B♭m Review

1st Position

3rd Position

6th Position

10th Position

© 2008 Mel Bay Publications (BMI). All Rights Reserved.

Bad Times

Medium rock / blues

W. Bay

Obadiah Johnson

Lively tempo

W. Bay

© 2008 Mel Bay Publications (BMI). All Rights Reserved.

Ortega

W. Bay

Latin jazz feeling

© 2008 Mel Bay Publications (BMI). All Rights Reserved.

Ortega (cont.)

Waves

Medium jazz rock

W. Bay

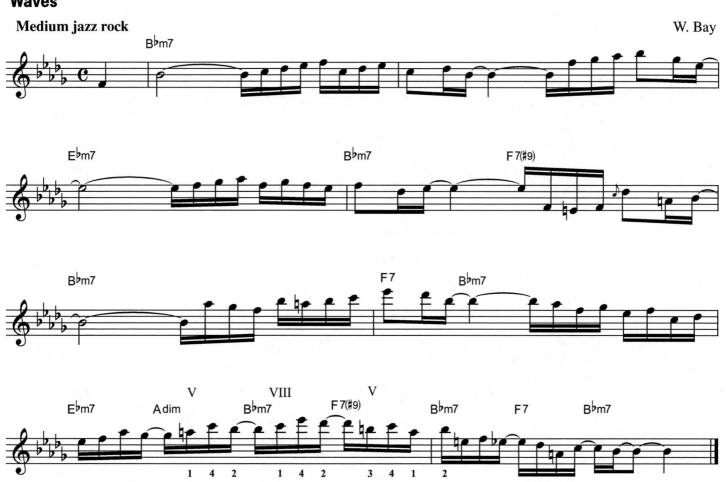

© 2008 Mel Bay Publications (BMI). All Rights Reserved.

Position Etude in B♭ Minor (6th Position)

Lazy Evening

Guitar Solo

Mel Bay

© 2008 Mel Bay Publications (BMI). All Rights Reserved.

Chords in the Key of B♭m

© 2008 Mel Bay Publications (BMI). All Rights Reserved.

Bbm Scale Harmonized

Chord Studies in Bbm

© 2008 Mel Bay Publications (BMI). All Rights Reserved.

© 2008 Mel Bay Publications (BMI). All Rights Reserved.

Bb m Quartal Harmony
Using the Pure Minor Scale

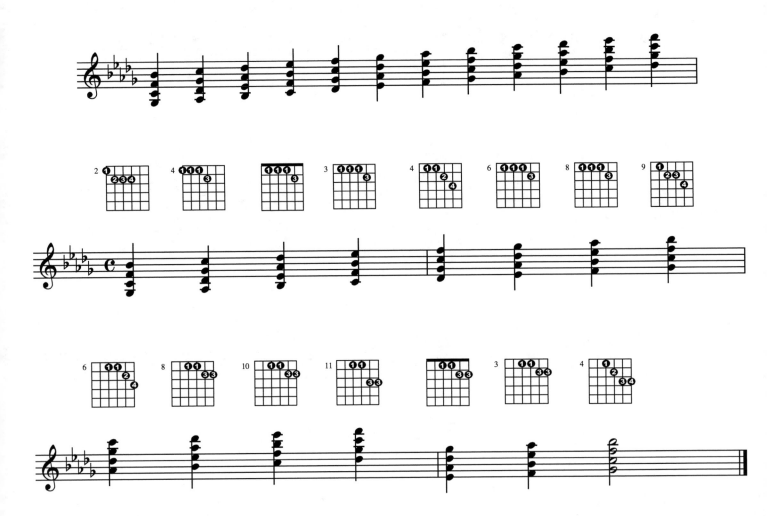

© 2008 Mel Bay Publications (BMI). All Rights Reserved.

B♭m Quartal Harmony Studies

© 2008 Mel Bay Publications (BMI). All Rights Reserved.

Key of B♭m Triad Studies

© 2008 Mel Bay Publications (BMI). All Rights Reserved.

Film Noir

Dropped D Tuning
Slowly

William Bay

© 2008 Mel Bay Publications (BMI). All Rights Reserved.

The Eleventh Chords

The eleventh chord consists of a root, major third, perfect fifth, minor seventh, major ninth, and major eleventh intervals.

Example

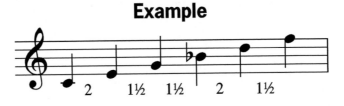

The Note-Spelling of the Eleventh Chords

The Eleventh Forms

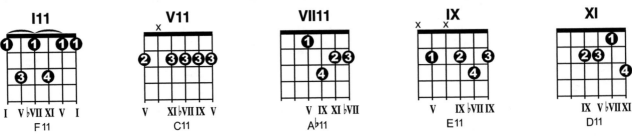

*The Roman numerals at the botton of the chords indicate the chordal tone.

The easiest and most direct way to create a eleventh chord on the fingerboard is by raising the third of a seventh or ninth chord one half step. The third then becomes the eleventh tone. Note the absence of the third in all but one eleventh forms above.

© 2008 Mel Bay Publications (BMI). All Rights Reserved.

The Orchestral Forms

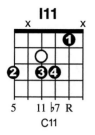 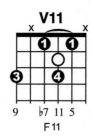 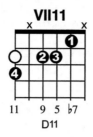 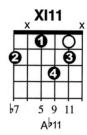

I11	V11	VII11	IX11	XI11
5 11 ♭7 R	9 ♭7 11 5	11 9 5 ♭7	5 11 ♭7 9	♭7 5 9 11
C11	F11	D11	B11	A♭11

> The white circle indicates the 3rd.

The Inside Eleventh Forms

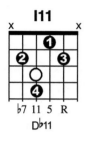 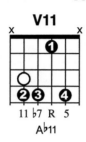 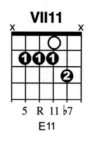 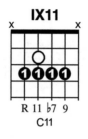 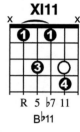

I11	V11	VII11	IX11	XI11
♭7 11 5 R	11 ♭7 R 5	5 R 11 ♭7	R 11 ♭7 9	R 5 ♭7 11
D♭11	A♭11	E11	C11	B♭11

The 7sus4 chord is a substitution for the 11th.

> Play all the above chords chromatically, playing two beats as an eleventh, and resolving the eleventh tone to the third, thus converting back to a seventh or ninth, depending upon the form used.

No Excuse

Medium latin rock

W. Bay

© 2008 Mel Bay Publications (BMI). All Rights Reserved.

Key of G♭ Review

G Flat Scale – 1st Position

Solution – 1st Pos.

W.B.

G Flat Scale – 6th Position

Terra Cotta – 6th Pos.

W.B.

© 2008 Mel Bay Publications (BMI). All Rights Reserved.

Key of G♭ Review

© 2008 Mel Bay Publications (BMI). All Rights Reserved.

Key of G♭ Review

1st Position

6th Position

8th Position

11th Position

© 2008 Mel Bay Publications (BMI). All Rights Reserved.

Flower Song

Guitar Solo

Lange
Arr. by Mel Bay

Lento moderato

cantabile

rit.

a tempo

Fine

D.S. al Fine

rit.

© 2008 Mel Bay Publications (BMI). All Rights Reserved.

The Key of F# Major

F# major is enharmonic to G♭ major. There are 6 sharps in F#. There are F#, C#, G#, D#, A# and E#.

The F# and G♭ Scales in the First Position

F# Scale in 3 Octaves

Speed Study

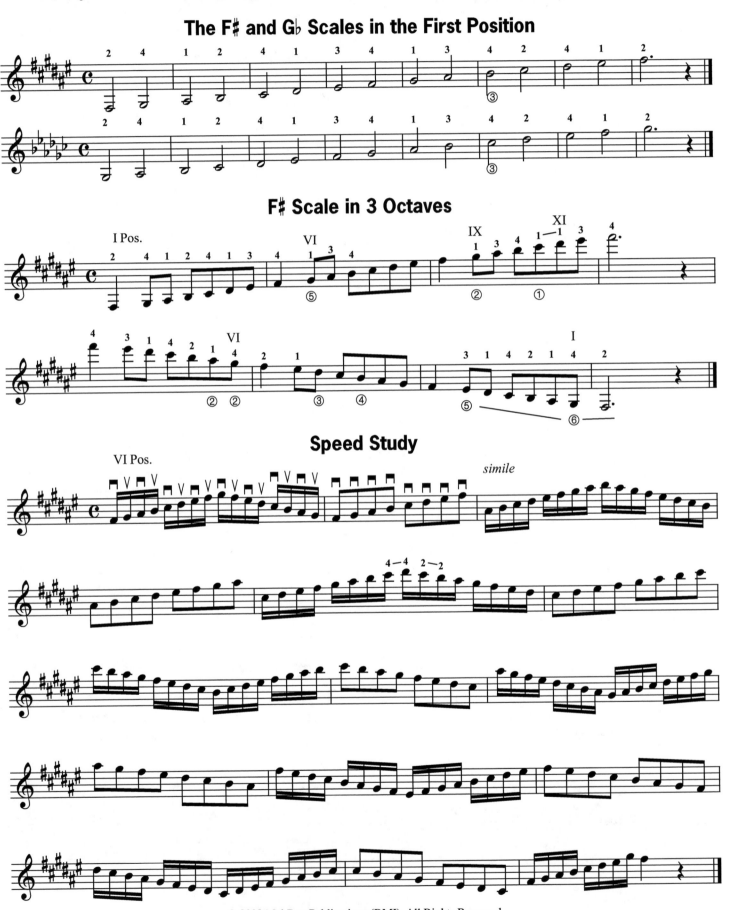

© 2008 Mel Bay Publications (BMI). All Rights Reserved.

Chords in the Key of G♭

© 2008 Mel Bay Publications (BMI). All Rights Reserved.

Gb Scale Harmonized

Chord Studies in Gb

© 2008 Mel Bay Publications (BMI). All Rights Reserved.

© 2008 Mel Bay Publications (BMI). All Rights Reserved.

Gb Quartal Harmony

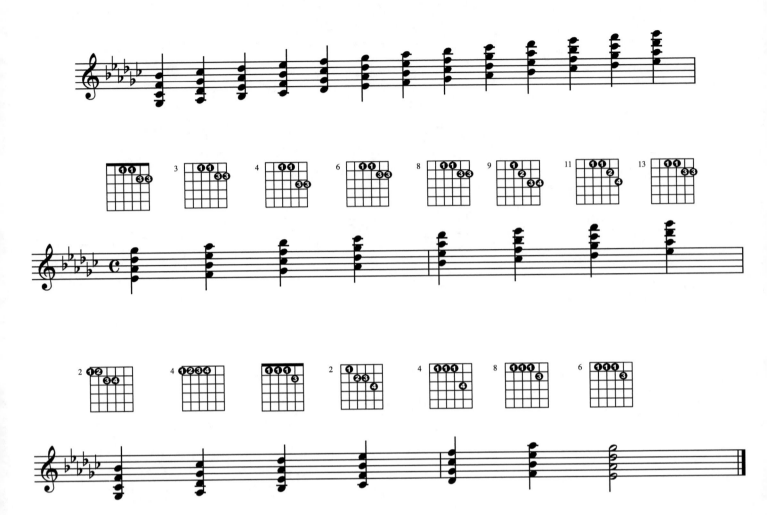

© 2008 Mel Bay Publications (BMI). All Rights Reserved.

G♭ Quartal Harmony Studies

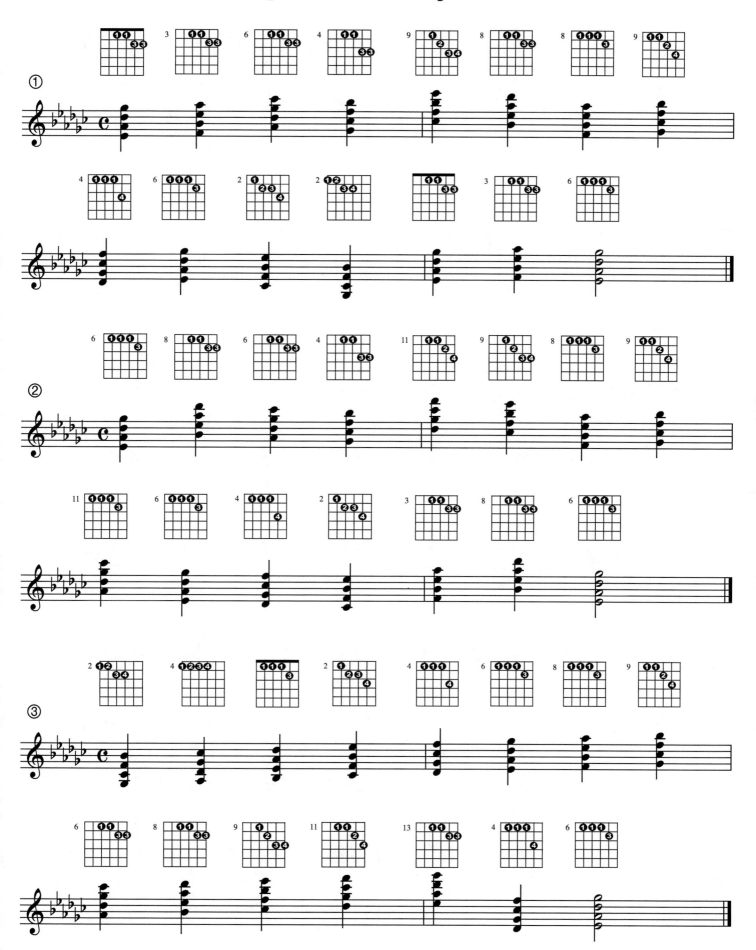

© 2008 Mel Bay Publications (BMI). All Rights Reserved.

Key of G♭ Triad Studies

© 2008 Mel Bay Publications (BMI). All Rights Reserved.

Key of E♭m Review

E Flat Minor Scale / Harmonic Mode – 3rd Position

Minor Etude – 3rd Pos.

W.B.

E Flat Minor Scale / Harmonic Mode – 6th Position

Gypsy Echoes – 6th Pos.

W.B.

© 2008 Mel Bay Publications (BMI). All Rights Reserved.

Key of E♭m Review

E Flat Minor Scale / Harmonic Mode – 8th Position

© 2008 Mel Bay Publications (BMI). All Rights Reserved.

Key of E♭m Review

3rd Position

6th Position

8th Position

11th Position

© 2008 Mel Bay Publications (BMI). All Rights Reserved.

Theme from "Polish Dance"

Xaver Scharwenka
Arr. by Mel Bay

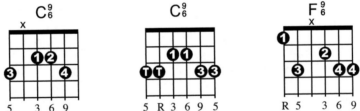

The Nine-Six Chord

Symbol: $^9_6$. The $^9_6$ chord is made by adding the ninth tone to the major sixth chord. It is played as the symbol indicates, the ninth over the sixth. There will be no inversions. The three practical forms are shown below:

The Minor Nine-Six Chord

This chord is created by lowering the third of the major nine-six chord a half step.

© 2008 Mel Bay Publications (BMI). All Rights Reserved.

The Keys of D♯ Minor and E♭ Minor

D♯ minor is enharmonic to E♭ minor.

The Harmonic Mode

Minorology

Guitar Solo
Lively

Mel Bay

© 2008 Mel Bay Publications (BMI). All Rights Reserved.

Chords in the Key of E♭m

© 2008 Mel Bay Publications (BMI). All Rights Reserved.

Eᵇm Scale Harmonized

Chord Studies in Eᵇm

© 2008 Mel Bay Publications (BMI). All Rights Reserved.

© 2008 Mel Bay Publications (BMI). All Rights Reserved.

E♭m Quartal Harmony
Using the Pure Minor Scale

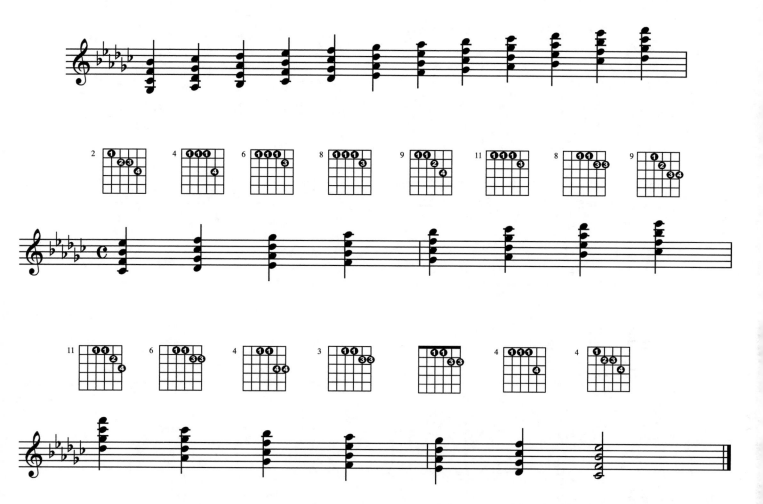

© 2008 Mel Bay Publications (BMI). All Rights Reserved.

E♭m Quartal Harmony Studies

© 2008 Mel Bay Publications (BMI). All Rights Reserved.

Key of E♭m Triad Studies

© 2008 Mel Bay Publications (BMI). All Rights Reserved.

The Thirteenth Chords

The thirteenth chord consists of the root, major third, perfect fifth, minor seventh, ninth, eleventh, and thirteenth intervals.

The Note-Spelling of the Thirteenth Chords

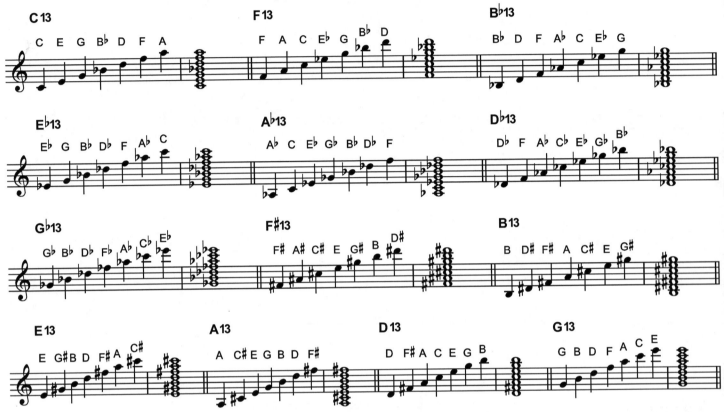

The Thirteenth Forms

Below are the best practical forms for effective playing:

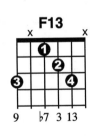 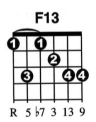 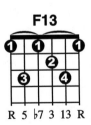 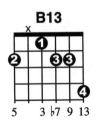 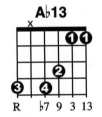

Play chromatically up the fingerboard for development.

© 2008 Mel Bay Publications (BMI). All Rights Reserved.